Australian Bush Fairies

Jan Wade

Published by
Murray Child & Company Pty Ltd
13 Lynwood Avenue, Dee Why, New South Wales, Australia 2099
Telephone: (02) 971 0067 Facsimile: (02) 982 4654
First published 1995
Reprinted (limp) 1996
© Jan Wade, 1995
Digital colour separation and film by Type Scan, Adelaide
Printed by South China Printing Company, Hong Kong

ISBN 0 908 048 29 7

This book belongs to:

Australian Bush Fairies

Jan Wade

MURRAY CHILD & COMPANY

The Native Violet

Mauve and white,
So sweet of face,
The Violet is a fairy place,
Where friends may meet and talk all day
In a finch and fairy way.

Little bird so small and light
With spotted wings of black and white,
Fly at sunset to your nest,
And there in safety
Take your rest.

The Ivy-leaf or Native Violet is a creeping herb which is widespread in the damp forests and woodlands of the coast and tablelands of Queensland, South Australia, New South Wales, Victoria and Tasmania.

The Double-barred or Owl-faced Finch is found across northern and eastern Australia. These pretty birds feed on various grass seeds and insects, are very sociable and remain in small flocks. Often the nests are built next to wasps' nests so any intruder will also disturb the wasps. This gives added protection to the clever little finch.

The Swamp Lily

White and spidery
Flowers bloom
In our swamplands
Misty gloom.
Star-like clusters
'mid twilight scene
Are home for fairies
Kind and serene.

Snowy lily, growing wild
You are the forest
And swamplands child.

A large bulbous herb, the Swamp or Crinum Lily grows in wet, swampy sites and in the rainforests of coastal Queensland and New South Wales. Its attractive flowers make it a favourite of Australian gardeners.

The Koala

Who is our favourite?
Who is the best?
Who do we love above the rest?
A furry bundle with shiny nose,
With fluffy ears and clinging toes.

Our koala is the one
And when the night has just begun
Eucalyptus leaves he'll eat
And gumtree fairies stop to greet.

The Koala is a marsupial whose young are born very tiny and spend a lengthy period growing in the mother's pouch before becoming independent. They feed on large amounts of certain Eucalypt leaves including the Manna Gum, Grey Gum, River Red Gum and Sydney Blue Gum and spend as much as nineteen hours of each day sleeping.

While the Koala is Australia's favourite animal, it may soon become a rare sight in our bushland. Hunting, disease, feral animals and land clearing have all decreased Koala numbers since European settlement.

The lofty Mountain Grey Gum is found in Victoria and New South Wales. The tree is large for home gardens but is often seen in parks. When the bark is shed an attractive yellow, grey and white surface is revealed.

The Mallee Rose

The spider spins his silken web,
A fairy finds her rest,
The silver palace in the sky
Becomes the robin's nest.

Frosty leaves of the Mallee Rose
Enfold red flowers grand,
This ornamental shrub is seen
Throughout our western land.

The Red-capped Robin is found in the
interior and sometimes in mid-western
Australia. These little birds feed on insects
and build very decorative nests of moss and
bark. Spider webbing is used to bind the
nest together.

The Mallee Rose with its silver-grey
leaves and large red flowers grows mainly
in Western Australia. The flowers occur
throughout the year and the species is
drought resistant.

The Native Myrtle

Tiny warrior, fierce and bold,
Of battles and great deeds untold,
Scamper across the shadowed lands,
By Native Myrtles and silver sands.
Night hunter, fairy steed,
Continue on your quest with speed.

The Common Dunnart is a mouse-sized
marsupial insect-eater. These fierce nocturnal
hunters rest during the day in nests of dried
grass in hollow logs. The Common Dunnart is
only one of about ten species of Dunnart in
Australia. Some have become rare but others
in remote or desert regions are still common.

An erect bushy shrub, the Native Myrtle
or Water Bush grows in sandy soils along dry
inland rivercourses and rocky gorges.
Flowering in winter and spring it is found
in all mainland states.

The Brown Boronia

Fairy scent upon the air
Will take away your every care,
Floating sweet on the springtime breeze,
Amongst the flowers
And the trees.

"Egg and bacon", the children say,
As in the wind they watch them sway.
Brown Boronia, you must be
The sweetest flower treat for me.

The wonderfully strong and sweet perfume of the Brown or Sweet-scented Boronia is unmistakeable in the Australian bush during its flowering period in late winter and spring. Because of its colouring this Boronia is often called the "egg and bacon plant".

The Couch Honeypot

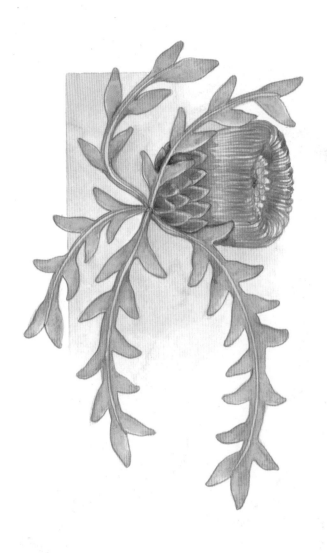

Small as a mouse
With a long, long tail
The Honey Possum
Looks tiny and frail,
But with sharp eyes
And a pushy snout
He'll seek the sweetest nectar out.

See the fairies' honey pot
With petals of spun gold?
They'll share this place
With furry friends
And bushland stories
Will be told.

The Honey Possum is a tiny marsupial
which lives on the nectar of wild flowers.
This little animal is a nimble climber and often
hangs upside down when feeding. Sometimes
it shelters in abandoned birds' nests but often
builds its own. The Honey Possum is found
only in south-western Australia and has no
relative anywhere in the world.

A low-spreading shrub, the Couch
Honeypot flowers in winter and spring and
grows in sandy and gravelly soils in south-
western Western Australia.

The Lemon Bottlebrush

Yellow brushes catch the light,
Lemon flowers sway,
The Bottlebrush, a feast for birds,
Brightens up our day.

Magic rainbows in the sky
The Lorikeets are passing by.
Colours flashing in the sun —
Just Lorikeets having fun.

An erect shrub or small tree, the Lemon Bottlebrush has yellow to cream brushes. Flowering in spring and summer it is found near watercourses in Queensland, New South Wales, Victoria and Tasmania.

Rainbow Lorikeets have adapted well to man's intrusion and are plentiful where suitable trees for nesting have been left. Lorikeets feed on the pollen and nectar of flowering Eucalypts, Grevillea and Banksia. They nest in tree hollows and both parents feed the young. These wonderful birds become very tame and trusting and people find it tempting to feed them. However, they will stay healthier and live longer if you just provide fresh water and plant suitable flowering shrubs in your garden.

18

The Spotted Gum

Spotted Gum so straight and tall
Reaching for the sky,
Watch the stars
And catch the wind
And see the clouds roll by.

Sugar Glider of the night
Take me on your fairy flight
Above the bush
Below the moon
So I can hear the bushland tune.

An attractive tree of coastal New South Wales and
south-eastern Queensland, the Spotted Gum has a
smooth bark which changes colour giving a beautiful
spotted or mottled appearance.

The Sugar Glider has a membrane on each side of
its body which it spreads to enable it to glide 45
metres or so from tree to tree in search of food or to
escape danger. The diet of the glider includes the
nectar of flowering trees and the sap of some
Eucalypts. A very active animal, the Sugar Glider is
nocturnal and is found in Eucalypt forests from the
Northern Territory to South Australia and Tasmania.

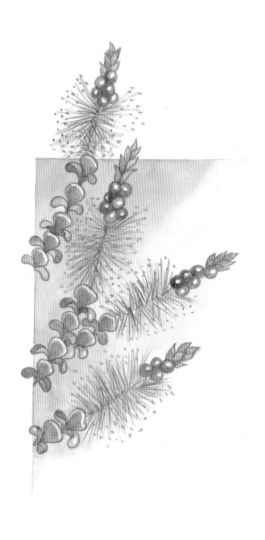

The Honey Myrtle

Chatter, chatter, parrot talk,
"I have a lot to say,
I've been busy flying round
On this hot and sunny day."

It's Oh! so nice to stop and chat
And talk with fairy folk,
To sit on Honey Myrtle
And share a parrot joke.

Cockatiels are found throughout most of inland Australia. They prefer open country where they are seen in trees along the edge of watercourses. These handsome little parrots are nomadic and eat the seed of various grasses and plants. The breeding season is August to December when four to seven white eggs are laid.

The Slender Honey Myrtle thrives in the heaths and open forests of New South Wales, Victoria, South Australia and Tasmania. Flowering occurs in spring and summer.

22

The Bilby

Into the desert lands you've fled
And these are all too dry,
When you have gone,
Will you be missed?
Will there be just me to cry?

Little friend, we're losing you,
You have become so rare,
But, still, there is some time for us,
If people will but care.

The Bilby with its long, soft blue-grey fur and delicate features seems out of place in the harsh deserts in which it now must live.

Once inhabiting large areas of mainland Australia, it is now restricted to desert regions of central Australia and a few scattered colonies in Western Australia. Feral animals and habitat destruction have contributed to the Bilby's decline. This nocturnal animal spends the hot days in its burrow, emerging after dark to feed on insects, seeds, bulbs and fungi found around the hummock grasslands and acacia shrublands in which it lives.

The Thorn Acacia is an erect, prickly shrub flowering in winter and spring on the dry rocky ridges of inland New South Wales, South Australia and the Northern Territory.

The Dagger Hakea

Soft and gentle little dove,
Your hat looks really grand.
How pleased we are
To know that you
Live right across our land.

The Hakea is a prickly chap,
Seems not a place to rest
But many birds will choose him
For he'll protect their nest.

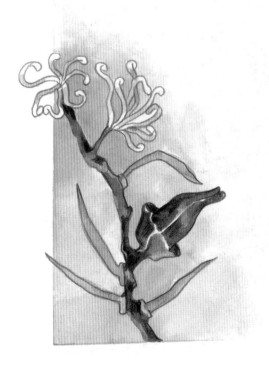

The Crested or Topknot Pigeon is one of Australia's twenty-four native pigeons and doves. Found over most of Australia they often visit suburban gardens and country homesteads. The Crested Pigeon feeds entirely on the ground, mainly on grass seeds and caterpillars. Breeding occurs during spring and summer when two eggs are laid.

The hardy straggling Dagger Hakea lives in damp, sandy soils in the coastal heaths and scrubs of New South Wales, Victoria and Tasmania. Many birds build their nests in the protection of its needle-like foliage.

Rock or King Orchid

Living in the forest
Clinging to a tree,
Clambering on a mossy rock,
Creamy Orchids I can see.

Below upon the forest floor
Two handsome frogs, bright green,
Their manners are impeccable,
The best a fairy's seen.

Growing on trees and rocks in forests and rainforests of the coast and tablelands of Queensland, New South Wales and Victoria, the Rock or King Orchid flowers in autumn, winter and spring.

The Green Tree Frog is one of our most common and attractive frogs. It has a soft, moist, brilliant green skin and is found along the coastal fringes to the drier interior regions of Western Australia, the Northern Territory, Queensland, South Australia and New South Wales.

29

The Kangaroo Apple

Little fellow on my lawn,
The prettiest wren in town.
Jewel-like bird
Dressed in blue,
Turquoise, black and brown.

In my basket I will gather
All the fruit I'm able,
Orange berries, flowers blue
For a fairy table.

The male Superb Fairy Wren's plumage becomes
brilliant blue in the breeding season to attract
females. The female is brownish in colour and both
parents share in the duties of caring for the young.
Insects and tiny seeds are the main diet. These pretty,
common garden birds are often seen darting across
suburban lawns in southern Queensland, New South
Wales, Victoria, South Australia and Tasmania.

The flowers of the Kangaroo Apple are blue or
violet and the fruits are orange berries. They are
found in forests and rainforests in Queensland, New
South Wales and Victoria and flowering occurs in
spring and summer.